Therapy

Gratitude Therapy

written by
Christine A. Adams

illustrated by
R.W. Alley

One
Caring
Place

Abbey Press

Text © 1999 by Christine A. Adams
Illustrations © 1999 by St. Meinrad Archabbey
Published by One Caring Place
Abbey Press
St. Meinrad, Indiana 47577

Library of Congress Catalog Number
99-73382

ISBN 0-87029-332-X

Printed in the United States of America

Foreword

At certain moments, gratitude comes easily. We are full to the brim with joy, and that feeling naturally spills over into thankfulness for the goodness and grace of our lives.

At other times, gratitude is nearly unthinkable—times of pain and illness, loss and grief, trouble and worry. How can we be thankful at times like these? Why *should* we be?

Author Christine A. Adams maintains that it is at the times we're tried and tested that we most need gratitude. For gratitude revives our inner core. It reminds us of better times and the bigger picture. It allows us to draw from the bottomless well of the soul, to summon the peace and power, hope and healing to get through.

In this little volume, you'll discover how and why to be grateful—always. You'll find techniques for realizing, renewing, and reflecting all the goodness in your life. You'll find how to "store up" gratitude, as a kind of savings account against the inevitable times of spiritual bankruptcy.

We already possess all we need to be happy and at peace—the awareness of who we are and what we have been given. This is gratitude!

1.

Gratitude is an attitude of the heart. Thankful people live each moment with a sense of wonder and contentment. Count your blessings and watch them grow!

2.

Gratitude is like a magnet attracting greater happiness, a more fulfilling life, and more satisfying relationships. Every day, let your heart fill with love. Gratitude creates more reasons to feel grateful.

3.

Start a Love List. Beginning today, when you see, hear, or experience something that brings tears of gratitude to your eyes, write it down. Over time you will begin to see a pattern emerging. This will help to clarify what really moves you and to motivate you in living a life that matters.

4.

Each day is alive with new possibilities. Each moment is an extraordinary gift. You are right where you are supposed to be right now. This moment is all you have. Cherish it!

5.

When you wake up, listen to the birdsong. Greet the day with a happy heart, knowing that just as God provides for the birds, God provides abundantly for you.

6.

As you go through the day,
be mindful of the little miracles
that grace your path. Celebrate
all the good around you and
within you.

7.

Slow your pace...and open your
senses to the world around you.
Notice the vivid beauty of
color—the brand-new-green of
spring leaves, the fathomless red
of a rose, the shimmering gold
of a misty morning. Become the
color you see. Look into nature's
secrets to find yourself.

8.

Listen to a butterfly flutter its wings. Stand near a waterfall and hear nature's applause. Throw your head back and let your soul rejoice to the song of the wind. Listen to the music of the universe.

9.

Hold still! Breathe in and out slowly, focusing on the life flowing through you. Let the silence hold you in its arms. Be still and know God.

10.

Before you sleep, thank God
for another day of life.
Rest—knowing you are loved,
you are blessed, you are held
tenderly in the hands of a
loving God.

11.

Watch the seasons change.
All things in nature change,
including you and your seasons
of life. Embrace change! God is
there in the barrenness, the new
beginnings, the fruitfulness,
and the changing colors of life.

12.

Eat slowly, with gratitude for
the nourishment provided for
you. Delight in deliciousness.
Keep your body strong with
healthy food and exercise, for
your body is your instrument
of praise to the Creator.

13.

What is your most cherished dream? Write it on a small slip of paper and carry it with you every day, as you visualize your dream coming true. Be thankful for who you are today and who you will be tomorrow.

14.

Value every day by working at what you love. Don't wait until after you "get enough money" or when you "have the time" to do what you were made to do. Be grateful for your talents and choose to use them.

15.

Once you discover your life's
mission, you are on your
way to living the life you love.
An inspired purpose produces
courageous actions, which,
in turn, create success.
Commit to your calling
with specific action goals.

16.

Grateful thoughts are healthy thoughts. They keep us focused on our dreams and steer us in the direction of personal achievement. Tomorrow is the result of what you do, think, and believe today. Believe that life is good and it will be!

17.

When you reach an important goal, rejoice. Be thankful—for the confirmation of your dream, for your perseverance in making your dream come true. Hold onto the pure joy of that moment. Come back to it again and again.

18.

Acknowledge the people in your life: those you care about and those you dislike. Everyone you meet teaches you something. Be grateful for them and to them, because God is working <u>through</u> them.

19.

Positive thoughts are healthy thoughts. Opening our hearts to the unconditional love of God is the essence of healing. Listen to your thoughts. If you think and say things like "This job is killing me," "I can't stand him," or "She makes me sick," your mind will believe you. Think positive; be well.

20.

God loves you as you are
and is with you right now.
Reassure yourself, "I am perfect
in God's love." Speak "joy" to
any negative, critical thoughts
that crowd out gratitude.

21.

A sense of gratitude lets
you know that you are a
well-loved child of God. It
empowers you to choose
wisely—what you believe,
how you feel, what you say,
and what you do. Thank God!

22.

You cannot be thankful and unhappy at the same time; it's emotionally impossible. God's will for you is joy. Accept joy, and realize that everything that happens to you—"good" and "bad"—blesses you.

23.

Be grateful for the journey of life, with all its twists and turns, detours and diversions. We often learn much more from the rocky road than from the smooth path.

24.

Be thankful, even in the face of adversity and distress. At times like this, gratitude means turning our will over to God's greater plan. Gratitude enhances the colorful canvas of our lives by allowing us to see the larger picture.

25.

A thankful heart redirects the mind away from fear and despair toward the love of God. Fear sees limits; gratitude sees possibilities. Fill your heart with so many grateful thoughts that no room remains for worry and fear.

26.

As children, we may have
learned to believe that we
have all we need and deserve;
or we may have learned to feel
cheated, deficient, or helpless.
Even if you have felt unblessed
in the past, it's not too late to
grow grateful.

27.

Gratitude has great restorative powers. When you're feeling down or unappreciated, make a list of all the wonderful things in your life. Write a thank-you note to God. Soon you'll be smiling.

28.

If regrets from the past crowd into the present, remember that there are no mistakes—just lessons to be learned. All things work together for good for those who love God and believe in Providence.

29.

Helping others benefits them, makes you appreciate your own gifts, and improves your mood. You can do volunteer work on a regular basis or simply spontaneously engage in acts of kindness. Help yourself by helping others!

30.

Ingratitude brings a sense
of deprivation to our lives.
Resentment and victimhood
tend to repel others, so that we
experience less love and support.
Let go of bitterness; embrace
thankfulness for what you
have, who you are, and what
you've done with what you
were given.

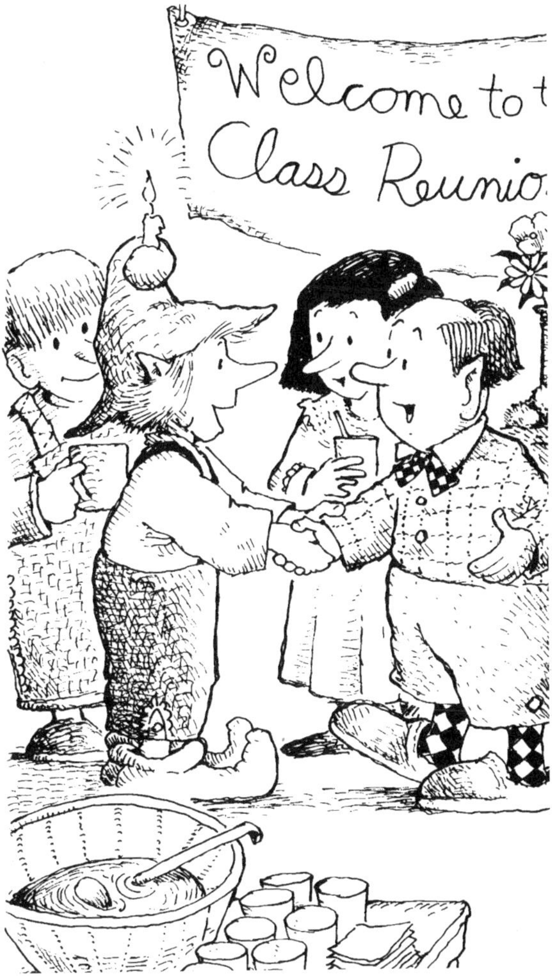
Welcome to t
Class Reunio

31.

When your heart is broken,
when a dream is shattered,
when you lose something or
someone important, it's hard to
feel grateful. Remember times
when you've felt the flow of
grace in your life. Allow the
gratitude from those times to
wash over you now. Trust that
God wants only good for you.

32.

Set aside some private moments for conversations with God. Ask for the inner wisdom to create solutions to any problems you face, and thank God for the help you know will come.

33.

Think of a situation that once appeared to be a problem but turned out to be a blessing in disguise. Think of a problem you are experiencing right now. List the ways you might ultimately benefit from this problem.

34.

Close your eyes and pretend you are watching your "life movie," beginning with the first day you remember. Bring the action up into the present day. Before opening your eyes, applaud yourself and the cast of people in your life.

35.

Tell those who help or serve you how appreciative you are. Tell salesclerks, waiters, postal workers, employees, friends, family, and perfect strangers. Share the gift of gratitude. Change the world!

36.

Say "Thank you!"—aloud, in a note, through a wave to a courteous motorist, via a gift. The person thanked will feel valued and appreciated. And when you make another person feel good, you feel good.

37.

The world needs you, and life is grateful for you. Honor your valuable contributions and talents, your productivity and energy, your words and deeds. Take a moment to feel thankful for the self-worth you already possess.

38.

Put your faith in God's guidance, protection, and endless love. Together with God, you can do all things. Be grateful for God! Be grateful for God in you!

Christine A. Adams is an internationally published writer, workshop leader, and national speaker. She is the author of the Elf-help book *One-day-at-a-time Therapy,* as well as *Living in Love* (Health Communications, Inc.) and *Holy Relationships* (Morehouse Publishing Group). She lives in California with her husband, Robert J. Butch.

Illustrator for the Abbey Press Elf-help Books, **R.W. Alley** also illustrates and writes children's books. He lives in Barrington, Rhode Island, with his wife, daughter, and son.

The Story of the Abbey Press Elves

The engaging figures that populate the Abbey Press "elf-help" line of publications and products first appeared in 1987 on the pages of a small self-help book called *Be-good-to-yourself Therapy*. Shaped by the publishing staff's vision and defined in R.W. Alley's inventive illustrations, they lived out author Cherry Hartman's gentle, self-nurturing advice with charm, poignancy, and humor.

Reader response was so enthusiastic that more Elf-help Books were soon under way, a still-growing series that has inspired a line of related gift products.

The especially endearing character featured in the early books—sporting a cap with a mood-changing candle in its peak—has since been joined by a spirited female elf with flowers in her hair.

These two exuberant, sensitive, resourceful, kindhearted, lovable sprites, along with their lively elfin community, reveal what's truly important as they offer messages of joy and wonder, playfulness and co-creation, wholeness and serenity, the miracle of life and the mystery of God's love.

With wisdom and whimsy, these little creatures with long noses demonstrate the elf-help way to a rich and fulfilling life.

Elf-help Books

...adding "a little character" and a lot
of help to self-help reading!

Gratitude Therapy
#20105 $4.95   ISBN 0-87029-332-X

Garden Therapy
#20116 $4.95   ISBN 0-87029-325-7

Elf-help for Busy Moms
#20117 $4.95   ISBN 0-87029-324-9

Trust-in-God Therapy
#20119 $4.95   ISBN 0-87029-322-2

Elf-help for Overcoming Depression
#20134 $4.95   ISBN 0-87029-315-X

New Baby Therapy
#20140 $4.95   ISBN 0-87029-307-9

Grief Therapy for Men
#20141 $4.95   ISBN 0-87029-306-0

Living From Your Soul
#20146 $4.95   ISBN 0-87029-303-6

Teacher Therapy
#20145 $4.95   ISBN 0-87029-302-8

Be-good-to-your-family Therapy
#20154 $4.95   ISBN 0-87029-300-1

Stress Therapy
#20153 $4.95   ISBN 0-87029-301-X

Making-sense-out-of-suffering Therapy
#20156 $4.95   ISBN 0-87029-296-X

Get Well Therapy
#20157 $4.95   ISBN 0-87029-297-8

Anger Therapy
#20127 $4.95   ISBN 0-87029-292-7

Caregiver Therapy
#20164 $4.95   ISBN 0-87029-285-4

Self-esteem Therapy
#20165 $4.95   ISBN 0-87029-280-3

Take-charge-of-your-life Therapy
#20168 $4.95   ISBN 0-87029-271-4

Work Therapy
#20166 $4.95   ISBN 0-87029-276-5

Everyday-courage Therapy
#20167 $4.95   ISBN 0-87029-274-9

Peace Therapy
#20176 $4.95   ISBN 0-87029-273-0

Friendship Therapy
#20174 $4.95   ISBN 0-87029-270-6

Christmas Therapy (color edition)
#20175 $5.95   ISBN 0-87029-268-4

Grief Therapy
#20178 $4.95   ISBN 0-87029-267-6

Happy Birthday Therapy
#20181 $4.95   ISBN 0-87029-260-9

Forgiveness Therapy
#20184 $4.95   ISBN 0-87029-258-7

Keep-life-simple Therapy
#20185 $4.95   ISBN 0-87029-257-9

Be-good-to-your-body Therapy
#20188 $4.95   ISBN 0-87029-255-2

Celebrate-your-womanhood Therapy
#20189 $4.95   ISBN 0-87029-254-4

Acceptance Therapy (color edition)
#20182 $5.95   ISBN 0-87029-259-5

Acceptance Therapy
#20190 $4.95   ISBN 0-87029-245-5

Keeping-up-your-spirits Therapy
#20195 $4.95   ISBN 0-87029-242-0

Play Therapy
#20200 $4.95   ISBN 0-87029-233-1

Slow-down Therapy
#20203 $4.95   ISBN 0-87029-229-3

One-day-at-a-time Therapy
#20204 $4.95   ISBN 0-87029-228-5

Prayer Therapy
#20206 $4.95   ISBN 0-87029-225-0

Be-good-to-your-marriage Therapy
#20205 $4.95   ISBN 0-87029-224-2

Be-good-to-yourself Therapy (hardcover)
#20196 $10.95   ISBN 0-87029-243-9

Be-good-to-yourself Therapy
#20255 $4.95   ISBN 0-87029-209-9

Available at your favorite giftshop or bookstore—
or directly from One Caring Place, Abbey Press
Publications, St. Meinrad, IN 47577.
Or call 1-800-325-2511.